MW01626401

for
Emmeline

By DR. TRUTH
THE NEW DEMOCRAT
As Related by Loren Spivack
Art Direction by Patrick Fields

For Glenn Beck
who inspires us all.

Published by: Free Market Warrior Publications.
Made in China.

This book is a work of parody that humorously represents numerous public figures past and present. It is not authorized by, endorsed by or affiliated with Glenn Beck or the Glenn Beck Program. It is not authorized by, endorsed by or affiliated with Theodor Geisel, his heirs or Dr. Seuss Enterprises.

Acknowledgments:

Leandro Martins Moraes: Illustration

Helena Babington Guiles, Babington.Co:
Book Design, Illustration and Graphic Editing

Orders, including bulk wholesale orders, and other inquiries:

www.obamaparody.com
obamaparody@gmail.com
718-614-4411

"I'm subversive as h***. 'The Cat in the Hat' is a revolt against authority, but it's ameliorated by the fact that the cat cleans up everything in the end. It's revolutionary in that it goes as far as Kerensky and then stops. It doesn't go quite as far as Lenin."

-Theodor Geisel (Dr. Seuss) 1986

The sun did not shine.
The Iraq war dragged on.
And our once great economy
Was almost all gone.

I sat there with Franklin.
We sat there, we two.
I wished, at that moment,
For somebody new.

Our political class
Kept expanding the state.
And the health of our country
Was quite far from great.

So all we could do was to

Fret

Fret

Fret

Fret!

We did not like Bush!
And didn't care whom we'd get!

Then someone yelled "CHANGE."
How that "change" sounded strange.

We looked at the TV
And saw him thereat.
We looked!
And we saw him!
A new Democrat!
And he said to us,
"Why are you frowning like that?

“I know you are poor
And the outlook’s not sunny,
But we can have fun
With other people’s money!

“I know some good games we could play,”
Said that cat.
“I know some good tricks,”
Said the New Democrat.

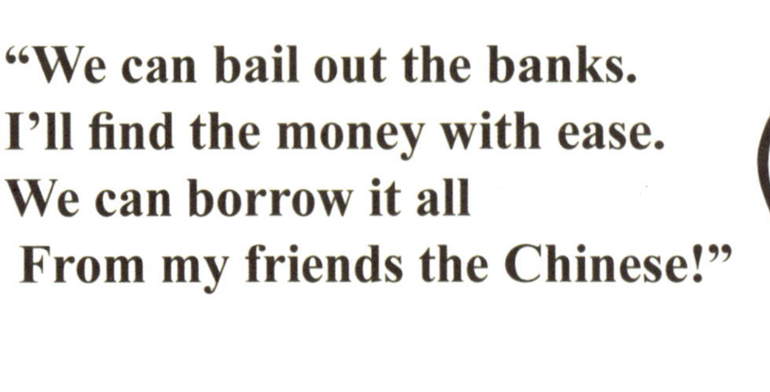

"We can bail out the banks.
I'll find the money with ease.
We can borrow it all
From my friends the Chinese!"

2nd Mortgage
U.S.A.
3RD MORTGAGE

**Then Franklin and I
Did not know what
to say.**

**The voters don't want
To be governed this way!**

Then Glenn said, "No! No!
Make that fool go away!
Tell that Democrat Cat
That your grandkids will pay
For his profligate spending,
His lust for power and pelf.
He's not helping you.
He only cares for himself!"

“Now! Now! Have no fear.”
Said that agent of ‘hope.’
“My plans are not bad.
You have to stop saying: ‘nope!’

We can stimulate everyone,
If only you let,
With a game that I call
Up-UP- UP with the debt!”

We must squander trillions.
(They wont ask where it went!)
If we don’t, unemployment
Might reach eight percent!

"Cut that out!,"
said old Glenn.
"This is not a sound plan.
You can't bring prosperity
To a country or man

By just handing out cash
When there's nothing
produced!
Only when the power
Of production is loosed

Can you hope to give our
General welfare a boost!"

“Have no fear” said the cat.
“I know just what to do.
I’ll take over GM
And then Chrysler too!
Then the people who make
The post office so fast
Will make your new car,
Since your old one won’t last!
With my ‘cash for clunkers’
You’ll be paid to destroy
You’re old SUV
So that we can employ
More union workers
Whose votes aren’t in doubt.
And when it all falls apart,
We’ll just bail them out!

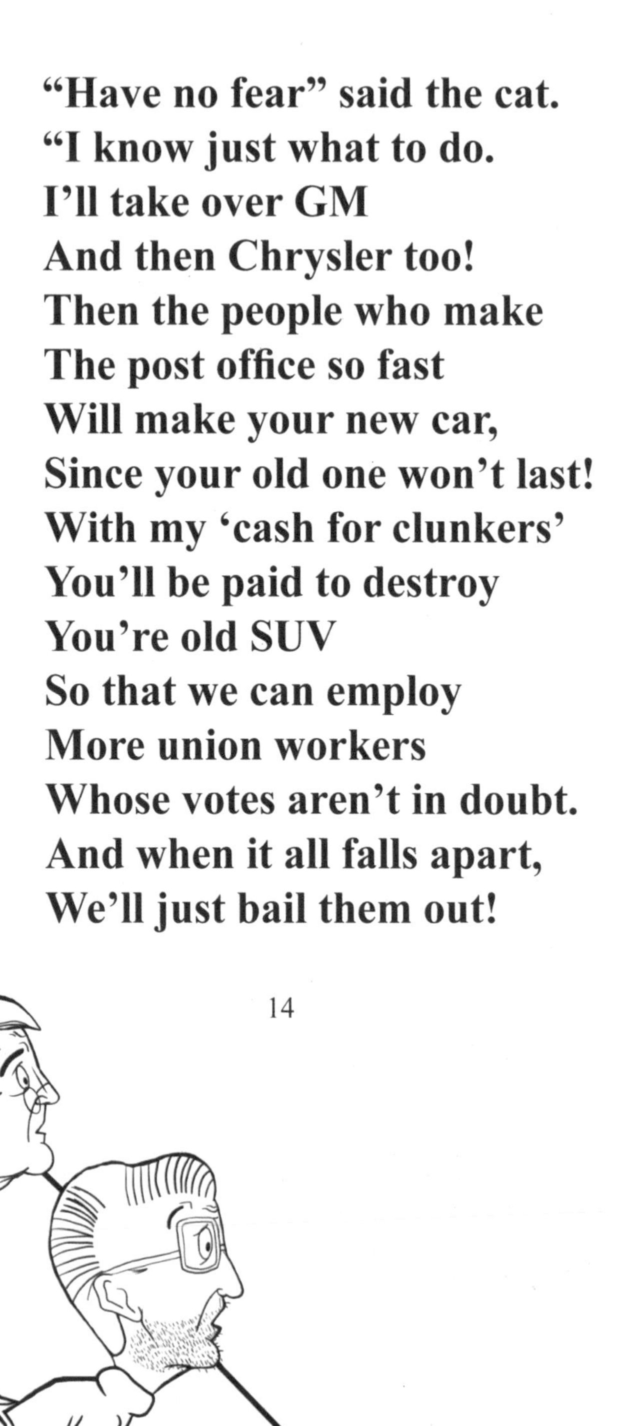

RULES
FOR
RADICALS
UAW
Oh, the Places
You'll
Go!

"I can change all the
things
That once made us great.
And if you disagree
Why, you're just filled
with hate!

"Yes, I'll pay for my votes
With the money I tax.
But that is not all I do!
Just sit back and relax…

"I'll build myself up
And make America small.
But that is not all!
No, that is not all!

"I'll make friends with our enemies.
They'll do us no harm...
If they see we are weak.
We must therefore disarm!

Did you think you saw
My foreign policy explode?
Well those dead Americans
Are just bumps in the road!"

“I’ll grovel to dictators
And bow to their kings.
Who cares about dignity?
I’ll just kiss their rings!

“Look at me!
Look at me!!
Look at ME
NOW!!!
It’s fun to win
prizes.
But you have to
know how.

"So I got the Nobel
Without doing a thing!
Then ran out of town,
Skipping lunch with the King."

"But they all hate George Bush
So they voted for me.
The same as you all.
Now we'll see what will be..."

Pussy Cat, Pussy cat
Where have you been?
"Sending an iPod…
A gift for the Queen!"

It was such a great gift,
(Though I don't like to boast!)
That I came back again,
And screwed up the toast!"

**"Now let me be clear,
It's not just us that I hate.
But also our allies
Who thought we were great,
Before I came to power.
So that means they're bad!
And they better not make
My friends the dictators mad!**

"Cause we don't need allies
Anymore. Don't you see?
All that America
Now needs is ME!"

US
Auto Sales
WORST ON
RECORD
STOCKS
TANK

And boy Glenn was angry!
His collar was hot!
He said, “Do I like this?
Oh, no! I do not!

“Now look what you’ve done!”
Said old Glenn to the cat.
“Look at our country!
It’s being laughed at!

“Your stimulus plan
Has made things much worse.
Our whole economy
Is now in reverse!

“We’re so deep in debt,
That we’ll never get out.
And you’ve emboldened our enemies!
We have no more clout.

"Our Founding fathers
Would turn in their graves,
If they could see now
How their successor behaves.

"Who would stay
on this course,
As our country derails?!?
I can only just pray
And hope that he fails!"

"But I like what I'm doing.
Oh I like it a lot!
And I'm just fulfilling
What Alinsky has taught.

"I don't wish to stop.
In fact, I'll do more!"
Said the New Democrat
As he rushed to the door.

And then he ran out
And came back with a box.
It was painted all red,
With a couple of locks.

IF I RAN The ZOO
BY Dr. Seuss

**"Now see what's in here!"
Said the cat with a smirk.
"I've got some small friends
To help with my work."**

**"Like me, they're committed
To seize every chance
To change our fair country
Into something like France!"**

IF I RAN The ZOO
By Dr. Seuss

**Then he unlocked the locks.
And out came his crew.
"Perhaps you should meet
Dem One and Dem Two."**

And they ran to us fast
And said, "Now for real fun!
You are going to be governed
By Dem Two and Dem one!"

Well, Franklin and I
Could not think what to do.
And they looked pretty harmless,
That Dem One and Dem Two.

But Glenn yelled, "No! No!
Those Dems should not be
Running our country.
You must believe me!

"We can't trust our freedoms
To this radical pair.
We must vote them out!"
Said Glenn, near despair.

“Have no fear,” said the Cat
“These are good little Things.
They just do what I say,
‘Cuz I pull the strings.

“And, as everyone knows
There’s so much to be done
So, first we must confiscate
Every single last gun.

“Cuz I think that it’s perfectly
Plain, don’t you see,
That no one should be armed
Unless they’re guarding a politician like me!

“Now here is a game
That they like,” said the Cat.
“They want to run healthcare
And chip away at...

**“Your freedom of choice.
‘Cuz they know what’s best
For you and your family.
Please don’t try to protest!**

**“Of course, it might mean
That Grandma must go.
(Our friendly “Death Panel”
Will be letting you know.)**

DEM 1
DEM 2

"The very best of technology
Will make everything right!
And Michelle had a friend
Who can design the website.

I know that Ted Cruz
was expressing some fear he had,
But I give you my word
you can keep your plan PERIOD!"

"Still my scheme isn't popular.
So, guess what we'll do?
We'll be bribing your Congressman
To vote against you!

A new bridge to nowhere,
A trip to Brazil,
Some retirement cash,
And you'll foot the bill!

"No! Not our healthcare!"
Said Glenn from his post.
"Without freedom there,
Our whole country is toast!

Our doctors will then be
Enslaved to the state;
With government bureaucrats
Deciding our fate."

Those Dems got to work;
And they got to work quick.
Tore up the Constitution
And then gave it a kick!

They banged it around
From the ceiling to floor.
And said "It's a living document!"
Glenn said "Not any more!"

They undermined the freedom
On which our republic depends.
And took tax payers' money
To spend on their friends.

We the
People
DE
DEM
1

Then Franklin and I
Heard them shout, "'Cap and trade!'
Is our chance to raise taxes
Whenever CO2s made."

"Wouldn't that include breathing?"
Glenn was cracking his voice.
"You're catching on fast!
But we have no choice.

"We'll stop global warming
By killing the jobs
Of working class people.
(Besides, they're all greedy slobs!)

"Just because there's been cooling
For ten or more years,
Can't stop us from pandering
To environmentalist fears.

"And families won't be able
To heat their house when it's cold.
Further reducing
Our need to care for the old!"

Then I saw a gleam
In the eye of Dem Two.
"Immigration reform
Is what we must do!"

“There are millions here
Who have broken our laws.
They snuck in our country.
But we’ll win their applause...
If we make them all legal.
Then guess how they’ll vote?”

“I’m touched!” said Dem One,
with a lump in her throat.
“Beside which,” she said
Who else would vote for us now?
They all know we wreak havoc
And our oaths disavow.

PRINT
TEA PARTY TAX RETURNS
STATE OF HAWAII
CERTIFICATION OF LIVE BIRTH
Stanley Ann Dunham
Mother
Barak Obama
Child
August 4, 1961
Date of Birth
John Smith
August 4, 1961
DEM 1
EARTH IN THE BALANCE By AL GORE
DEM 2
CHURCHILL
TO: MEXICAN DRUG CARTEL
Property of Blago

DEM 1
DEM 2
Did my revolt in '57
launch us all toward the abyss?
Certainly no cleanup job
can ameliorate this!

Then Glenn said, "Look! Look!"
And we all turned his way.
The voters were coming
For Election Day.

"Oh what will they do to us?
What do they want?"
Said Dem One to Dem Two
With The Cat nonchalant.

"Do something fast, Cat," said Dem One. "Don't you know?
The voters are coming! And they're not coming slow!"

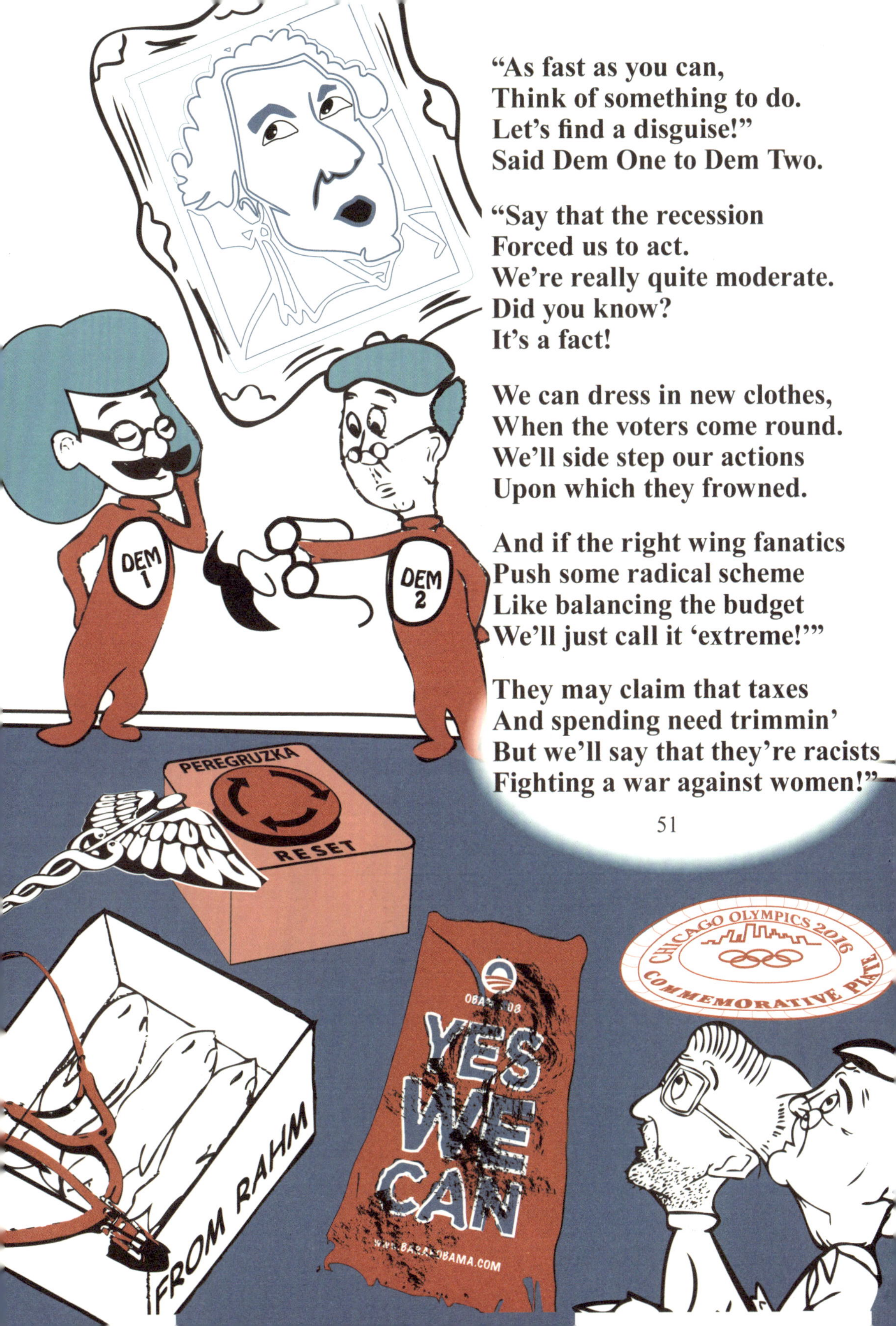

**"As fast as you can,
Think of something to do.
Let's find a disguise!"
Said Dem One to Dem Two.**

**"Say that the recession
Forced us to act.
We're really quite moderate.
Did you know?
It's a fact!**

**We can dress in new clothes,
When the voters come round.
We'll side step our actions
Upon which they frowned.**

**And if the right wing fanatics
Push some radical scheme
Like balancing the budget
We'll just call it 'extreme!'"**

**They may claim that taxes
And spending need trimmin'
But we'll say that they're racists
Fighting a war against women!"**

“Have no fear,” said the cat,
“The voters love me.
They’re just like the press.
I’m their Messiah, you see.
Those millions of people,”
He said, sounding flat,
“Want my ‘hope’
and my ‘change’.
I’m their new Democrat!”

“And I’ve been working so hard
To change everything,
And be their sole source of hope!
I’m their socialist king!
I know that they love me
I know their love never fails
Cuz I have the NSA
read all their emails!”

"I'm not so sure," said old Glenn.
"They look awfully mad.
Perhaps they just want
The freedoms they had!"

DONT TREAD ON ME
AMERICA STANDS UP!
TAKE
AMERICA
BACK

So America waited
On that cold, cold, wet day
To see what the voters
Would do with their say.

Would they learn to love socialism?
Keep the cat and his crew?
Or would they strike back for freedom?
What would you do?